Osip Mandelstam

POEMS

Second Edition

Translations by Ilya Bernstein

BOSTON • 2020

Osip Mandelstam. *Poems*
Translations by Ilya Bernstein

Second edition, revised, with an expanded commentary

ISBN 978-1950319244
Library of Congress Control Number: 2020940894

Earlier versions of some translations have appeared in *Persephone,
Circumference, Raritan Quarterly, Jubilat, Ars Interpres, Calque, Delos,
Osip Mandelstam: New Translations* (Ugly Duckling Presse, 2006),
Osip Mandelstam. Poems (M•Graphics, 2014).
A portion of the afterword has also appeared in *Delos*.

Cover Design by Paul Kraytman © 2014–2020

PUBLISHED BY M•GRAPHICS | BOSTON, MA

   www.mgraphics-publishing.com
   mgraphics.books@gmail.com

Printed in the United States of America

Table of Contents

◊ ◊ ◊

I was washing in the yard at night.
The stars in the sky were coarsely brilliant.
Not a ray, but salt thrown on an axe—
The barrel cool and full to overflowing.

All the gates are shut and fastened tight
And the earth is threaded-through with conscience.
What more pure foundation can there be
Than the truth of fresh and untouched canvas?

In the barrel, a star melts like salt,
And the water, cooling, becomes blacker—
Bitter fate more bitter, death more pure,
And more frightening the earth—and truer.

1921

◇ ◇ ◇

I know not when
This little song began—
Who scrapes along it, what thief?
What tinkling mosquito-prince?

I would like to talk
About nothing once more,
To scrape a match, to push
The night awake with my shoulder;

To throw haystacks and haystacks apart,
The wearisome weight of air;
To rend, to tear the sack
Where the caraway is packed.

So that the linkage of blood—
The tinkle of these dried herbs—
Once purloined, might be found
Across time, hayloft, and dream.

1922

◈ ◈ ◈

Up a little ladder I climbed
To a hayloft in utter disarray—
I inhaled the clutter of space,
The detritus of milky stars.

And I thought: Why awake
The swarm of drawn out sounds,
In this eternal wrangle why chase
Wondrous Aeolian scales?

The Big Dipper's stars are seven.
The earth's good senses are five.
The darkness swells and tinkles,
And grows and tinkles again.

A hay wagon, enormous, unyoked,
Athwart the universe stands.
The ancient chaos of the hayloft
Will tickle, prickle a man…

Not with our own skin's scales—
Against the hair of the world we sing.
We tune our lyres as if
Rushing to grow a fleece.

Scythemen restore to the nest
Finches that fall to the ground—
I will fly from furrows that burn
And return to my own row of sounds.

To make the linkage of blood
And the dried out tinkle of grass
Part ways: the one—made firm,
The other—a dream mirage.

1922

THE AGE

My age, my beast, who will discover
How to peer into your eyes
And with his own blood glue together
The vertebrae of two centuries?
Blood-the-builder gushes
From the throat of earthly things,
While a freeloader merely trembles
On the threshold of new days.

A creature must sustain its backbone
For as long as its life lasts,
And in an unseen spinal column
Undulates a playing wave.
Like a child's tender cartilage
Is the age of infant earth—
And like a lamb, life's headmost part
Has been sacrificed once more.

In order to free the age from bondage,
To begin the world anew,
The joints of days, gnarled and knotted,
Must be tied together by a flute.
It is the age that makes undulations
In the sorrow of human beings
And in the grass an adder breathes
Like a golden measure of the age.

Buds will swell again as always
And green sprouts will spurt,
But your backbone has been broken,
My wonderful pitiful age!
And with a meaningless smile,
You look backward, cruel and weak,
Like a beast that used to be agile,
On the tracks of your own feet.

Blood-the-builder gushes
From the throat of earthly things,
And the ocean's cartilage splashes
Its hot fish against warm shores.
And from the elevated bird net,
From the humid heaps of blue,
Indifference, indifference
Spills over your mortal wound.

1922

THE SLATE ODE

We will know only from the voice
What it was that scratched and struggled...

From star to star—a mighty bond,
The flinty path from the old ballad.
The flint, the air—their common tongue—
Flintstone and water—ring and horseshoe.
Upon the soft shale of the clouds
Appears a milky slate stone drawing—
Not the discipleship of the world,
But mere delirium of sheep dreaming.

We sleep upright in thickest night
And have a sheepskin hat to warm us.
The spring trickles back into the rock
In chains of speech that whirl and warble.
Written by fear, written by shifts,
Using a milky lead pencil,
This is the ripening rough draft
Of running water's own disciples.

Goat cities of the precipice,
The mighty layering of flintstones;
And even so, another ridge—
Sheep churches and habitations!

They heed the sermon of the plumb,
Water instructs them, time erodes them—
And they have saturated long ago
The air and its transparent forest.

Like a dead hornet beside the hive
The bright day is swept out in shame
And night-the-vulture carries back
Burning chalk and feeds the slate stone.
To erase the impressions of the day
From the iconoclastic panel
And like a chick to brush away
Visions that are already transparent!

The fruit matured. The grapes grew ripe.
The day raged as it always rages.
With gentle games of knucklebones
And with the coats of angry sheep dogs.
Like litter from the icy heights—
The underside of green impressions—
The hungry water runs,
Twisting and playing like an animal,

And like a spider it crawls toward me—
Where every bond is splashed by moonbeams,
On an astounding ascent,
I hear the shrieking of the slate stone.
I break the night, the burning chalk,
To make a hard immediate record,
I exchange noise for an arrow's song,
I tune my strings for strident fury.

Who am I? Not a mason, no,
And not a roofer or a shipwright —
A double-dealer, with twin souls,
Friend to the night, herald of the daylight.
Blessed is he who has called flint
A disciple of the running water,
And who has fastened, on solid ground,
Latchets around the feet of mountains.

And now I study the diary,
The scratches of a slate stone summer,
The flint, the air — their common tongue,
With sediments of light and darkness.
And I desire to thrust my fingers
Into the flinty path from the old ballad
As into a wound — to form a bond
Between flint and water — ring and horseshoe.

1923, 1937

◈ ◈ ◈

For the rattling valor of ages to come,
For the high tribe of men,
At the feast of the fathers I have forfeited my cup,
And my joy, and my honor as well.

A wolfhound-age leaps up on my back,
But I am not a wolf by blood.
Better find me a coat of Siberian steppes
And stuff me inside, like a hat...

Let me no more look at the coward, at the mire,
At the bloody bones in the wheel,
Let the blue foxes blaze the whole night through
In their primordial beauty for me.

Lead me into the night, where the Yenisei flows
And the pine tree reaches the star,
Because I am not a wolf by blood
And can only be killed by my like.

17–18 March 1931, end of 1935

CANZONE

Is it true that I will see tomorrow —
How my heart beats leftward, glory beating! —
You, the bankers of the alpine landscape,
You, the holders of the gneiss's assets?

With the eagle eye of a professor—
Egyptology and numismatics—
There are birds there that are sullen and crested
With tough meat and broad breastbones.

That is Zeus ingeniously adjusting
With his cabinet-maker's magic fingers
His extraordinary onion-glasses—
A gift to the seer from the psalmist.

He looks through those binoculars of Zeiss's—
A precious present from King David—
And makes out all of the gneiss's wrinkles,
Every pine tree, every gnat-sized village.

I will leave the land of the Hyperboreans
To saturate my destiny with eyesight.
I will say "selah" to the protector
Of the Jews for his raspberry kindness.

The unshaven mountains aren't clear yet,
And the stubble of the brushwood prickles,
And the valley is fresh, clean as a fable,
And green to the point of wincing.

I like field binoculars for giving
A compounding interest to vision.
Only two colors in the world have not faded:
Yellow jealousy and red impatience.

26 May 1931

LAMARCK

An old man there was — shy as a schoolboy —
An embarrassed, awkward patriarch…
Who will draw his sword for nature's honor?
Why, of course, the fiery Lamarck.

If all living things are merely scribbles
Cancelled in one transient, dying day,
Well then — on Lamarck's moveable ladder
Let me occupy the bottom rung.

To the ringed worms I'll descend and to the barnacles,
Brushing past the lizards and the snakes.
Over pliant planks and gullies
I'll decrease, like Proteus, and melt away.

I will wear a calcareous mantle,
My hot blood I will give up.
I will curl myself into the sea foam
And attach to it with suction cups.

We went past the orders of the insects
That have tiny shot glasses for eyes.
He said: all of nature is in fractures,
Vision ends — you see for the last time.

He said: let sonority be ended!
All your love for Mozart was in vain.
Usher in the silence of the spiders!
Here's a gap that lies beyond our strength.

And as if she didn't really need us,
Nature took her leave and stepped away.
And inside a scabbard she inserted,
As it were a sword, a long thin brain.

And the drawbridge she forgot to lower—
Was too late to lower for those who have
All the sinuosity of laughter,
And whose breath is red, and green their grave…

7–9 May 1932

◈ ◈ ◈

Oh, how we love to dissemble
And how easily we forget
That in our childhood we are nearer
Than in our riper years to death.

A sleepy child still holds a saucer
And from it slowly sips a grudge,
But I have nobody to pout at
And am alone on every road.

The beast will moult, the fish will frolic
In the oblivion of the waves—
Oh, that I might forget how skewed
Are human passions, human cares.

14 May 1932

TO THE GERMAN LANGUAGE

to B. S. Kuzin

> Freund! Versäume nicht zu leben,
> Denn die Jahre fliehn
> Und es wird der Saft der Reben
> Uns nicht lange glühn!
> *Ewald Christian von Kleist*

To my own ruin, to my own contradiction,
Like a moth flying toward a flame at midnight,
I want to make an exit from our language
For everything I owe to it forever.

There is between us praise without flattery,
And friendship to the hilt, without dissembling,
So let us learn some seriousness and honor
In the West, from a foreign family.

Poetry, you are well served by tempests!
I remember an officer, a German—
The handle of his sword was snared in roses
And on his lips was the name of Ceres…

The fathers in Frankfurt were still only yawning.
There was as yet no word of Goethe.
Hymns were composed, and horses capered
And pranced in place, like letters.

Tell me, my friends, in what Valhalla
Did you and I crack nuts together?
What kind of freedom was at our disposal?
What were the landmarks that you left me?

And directly from the page of a yearbook,
Directly from its firsthand freshness,
You stepped into the grave, unfearful,
As if going to the cellar for a bottle.

A foreign speech will be my outer skin,
And long before I dared to be born
I was a letter, I was a grapevine verse,
I was the book about which you dream.

When I slept without form or feature,
I was awakened by friendship, as by a gunshot.
God Nachtigall, give me the fate of Pylades
Or else pull out my tongue—I do not need it.

God Nachtigall, I am still being recruited
For new plagues, for seven-year slaughters.
The sound has narrowed, the words hiss and riot,
But you are alive, and with you I am undaunted.

8–12 August 1932

OCTAVES

I love the formation of tissue
When after two, after three,
Or after four attempts at inhaling
I draw an unbroken breath.

And using the arcs of racing
Sailboats to trace green shapes,
Like a child that has never known a cradle,
Space sleepily plays with itself.

November 1933, July 1935

❧

I love the formation of tissue
When after two, after three,
Or after four attempts at inhaling
I draw an unbroken breath.

And I feel so sweet and tormented
When that moment arrives
And suddenly an arc is extended
Through this muttering of mine.

November 1933 — January 1934

When, after destroying the sketches,
You diligently hold in your mind
A period not weighed down by glosses,
Intact in interior dark,

And nothing holds it together
But the pull of its own weight,
It relates to paper exactly —
As a dome to the empty skies.

November 1933 — January 1934

O butterfly, O Muslim maid,
Cut open in a shroud,
Lady Alive and Lady Dying,
So large — so you as you are!

A biter with such large whiskers
Bound up inside a burnous —
O shroud unfurled like a banner!
Fold your wings — dare I look?

November 1933 — January 1934

The saw-tooth paw of the maple
In the cup of a spandrel floats,
And pictures can be assembled
Out of butterflies' speckles on walls.

Certain mosques are alive
And I can now surmise:
Perhaps we are — Hagia Sophia
With countless numbers of eyes.

November 1933 — January 1934

Tell me, draughtsman of the desert,
Geometer of the Arabian sands,
Are lines, irrepressible, truly
More powerful than blowing wind?

"Its Judaic vexations
Never enter my mind."
He molds babbling into being
And from being babbling imbibes…

November 1933 — January 1934

Schubert in water, and Mozart in bird songs,
And Goethe whistling on the winding path,
And Hamlet reasoning with timid footsteps,
Measured the pulse of the crowd and believed the crowd.

Maybe before there were lips, there was already a whisper,
And leaves circled around in treelessness,
And those to whom we dedicate our learning
Prior to any learning acquired their traits.

November 1933—January 1934

Prevailing over nature's induration
The eye of harder blue inferred its law.
In the earth's crust minerals riot
And the cry strains at the breast like ore.

And the unhearing preformation labors,
Along a road that bends into a horn,
To understand space and its inner surplus—
Its implied petal, its implied dome.

January—February 1934

A minuscule sixth-sense appendage—
A lizard's parietal eye—
Or snails or oysters in their cloisters
Or what the shimmering cilia say—

The unattainable, at such close distance!
No looking, no unraveling allowed—
As if you have been handed a message
And have to answer it right now...

May 1932—February 1934

Out of bowls full of pins and pestilence
We swallow causality's lies.
With hooks we touch infinitesimals
As small as the lightest of deaths.

And where the spillikins have coupled
The child makes not a peep—
In little eternity's cradle
A big universe sleeps.

November 1933, July 1935

The neglected garden of magnitudes—
Into it, I step out of space.
The imaginary invariance
Of causes, I tear away.

And your textbook, infinity,
I read apart, by myself—
A leafless volume of remedies,
Of enormous roots to be solved.

November 1933, July 1935

◇ ◇ ◇

What street is this?
This is Mandelstam Street.
What an impossible name—
No matter which way you invert it,
It comes out crooked, not straight.

Little about him was straightforward.
His temperament wasn't perfect.
And that is why this street,
Or more precisely, this pit,
Has come to be known
By the name of this Mandelstam...

April 1935

◊ ◊ ◊

Yes, I lie in the earth, moving my lips,
And what I say will be repeated by every schoolboy:

The earth is nowhere as round as on Red Square,
And its ground is hard from voluntary roundness.

Nowhere is the earth as round as on Red Square,
And its roundness is spontaneously unbounded,

All the way to the rice fields sloping down—
As long as the last man on earth lives in bondage.

May 1935

◈ ◈ ◈

A wave like any other, that breaks the back of another,
Hurls itself at the moon with all the sorrow of bondage,
And the upswirling janissary water—
That citadel of sleepless undulations—
Curves over, crashes, and carves a pit in the sand.

And through the air, crepuscular and fleecy,
You seem to see a crenellated wall not yet begun
And the soldiers of suspicious sultans falling
From ladders of foam—detaching, splashing—
While eunuchs coolly pass poison around.

27 June—July 1935

◊ ◊ ◊

When, puffed up like brioche, the goldfinch
Begins to quake with quickening heart,
Rage peppers his scholastic gownlet
And how that cap of his looks smart!

The perch calumniates and slanders,
The cage outspeaks itself with slurs,
And inside out is the whole world
And there's a forest Salamanca
For clever, disobedient birds.

December 1936

THE BIRTH OF A SMILE

Whatever time a child begins to smile,
In one way bitterly, in one way sweetly,
The far ends of its smile, all jokes aside,
Are lost to sight in oceanic chaos.

The child feels an unconquerable joy.
With the corners of its lips it plays in glory
And a rainbow seam is already being stitched
For finding out what is reality.

Out of the water, land has risen on its paws—
The snail of the mouth washes up from under—
And one Atlantic moment strikes the eyes
Softly accompanied by praise and wonder.

9 December 1936 — 17 January 1937

◈ ◈ ◈

Not mine, not yours, but theirs — theirs is what strength
Reaches the ends of lineal descents:
Theirs is the air that vents the vocal reed
And gratefully the snails of human lips
Will draw from them a heaviness that breathes.

Name have they none. Enter into their grit
And you will become heir to their dominions.

And for human beings, for their living hearts,
Meandering in their volutes, their evolvements,
You will delineate what joys are theirs
And that which torments them — in tides, ebbing and flowing.

9–27 December 1936

◊ ◊ ◊

Idle inside a mountain an idol dwells
In protective, boundless, idyllic chambers,
While necklaces drip from his neck like drops of fat,
Protecting the ebb and flow of his slumber.

A peacock played with him when he was a boy
And he was fed on an Indian rainbow
And given milk out of rose-colored clay
And lavished with cochineal.

Somnolent bone has been tied in a knot.
Hands, knees, and shoulders have been made human.
He smiles with the quietest of mouths,
Uses his bones to think, uses his head to feel,
And struggles to recall his human features.

10–26 December 1936

◇ ◇ ◇

You're not dead yet, you're not yet all alone,
As long as with your beggar lady friend
You take delight in the majesty of plains
And in the gloom, the cold, the blowing snow.

In splendid indigence, in mighty poverty,
Live in tranquility and contentment.
Those days are blessed, blessed are those nights,
And the sweet labor of song is blameless.

He is unhappy who is cut low by the wind
And whom a dog's bark frightens like his own shadow.
And he is poor who, half alive himself,
Can only ask alms of a shadow.

15–16 January 1937

◇ ◇ ◇

What shall we do with the prostration of the plains,
Their drone of hunger and of wonder?
For that which we deem openness in them
Is what we see ourselves falling asleep,
And the question grows: where are they going,
        where have they been,
And could it be that he now crawls on them
Who is the one we scream about in our dreams—
The Judas of a mankind yet to be?

16 January 1937

◈ ◈ ◈

Do not compare: who lives is beyond compare.
Agreeing with the parity of the plains
I felt somehow caressed and scared,
And the sky's circle was my pain.

And I addressed my servant the air,
Awaiting tidings from him or service,
And I prepared to sail, and sailed along the arc
Of uninitiated journeys.

Where there's more sky for me, there I am ready to roam,
And it is clear despair that won't release me
From the Voronezh hills, which are still young,
To those of all mankind in Tuscany.

18 January 1937

◇ ◇ ◇

Today I'm in a spiderweb of light—
As if in black hair, and in fair—
What people need is light and air of blue
And they need bread and Elbrus Mountain snow.

And there is none who might enlighten me,
While I will hardly find one on my own:
Not in the Urals, not in the Crimea—
There are no such transparent, weeping stones.

The people need a poem mysteriously theirs,
To be awakened by it all their days
And in the sound of it to wash forever—
As in a flaxen curl, a nut-brown wave.

19 January 1937

◇ ◇ ◇

Where are the bound and fastened moans?
Where is Prometheus—the rock's support and buttress?
And where is the hawk—and the yellow-eyed burst
Of claws emerging from a lowered forehead?

All that is gone: tragedy is no more.
But these lips pressing themselves forward—
But these lips enter right into the core
Of Aeschylus the lader, of Sophocles the logger.

He is an echo and a hello, a milestone—no, a plowshare.
The stone-and-air theater of growing ages
Has risen to its feet, and everybody wants to see everybody—
Those who were born, the deathlings, and the deathless.

17 January—4 February 1937

◈ ◈ ◈

As a celestial stone awakens the earth somewhere,
An outcast poem has fallen, a poem that knows no father.
The unimplorable—a find for the creator—
Can be but what it is—none passes judgment on him.

January 20, 1937

[ODE TO STALIN]

If I were to employ charcoal for highest praise—
For the unalloyed gladness of a picture—
I'd cut up the thin air with the most subtle rays,
Feeling of care and of alarm a mixture.
So that the features might reflect the Real,
In art that would be bordering on daring
I'd speak of him who shifted the world's wheel,
While for the customs of a hundred peoples caring.
I'd raise the eyebrow's corner up a bit,
And raise it once again, and keep on trying:
Look how Prometheus has got his charcoal lit—
Look, Aeschylus, at how I'm drawing and crying!

I'd make a handful of resounding lines
To capture his millennium's early springtime,
And I would tie his courage in a smile
And then untie it in the gentle sunshine;
And in the wise eyes' friendship for the twin,
Who shall remain unnamed, I'll find the right expression,
Approaching which, you'll recognize the father—him—
And lose your breath, feeling the world's compression.
And I would like to thank the very hills
Which bred his hand and bone and gave them feeling:
Born in the mountains, he knew too the prison's ills.
I want to call him—no, not Stalin—Dzhugashvili!

Painter, guard and preserve the warrior with your paint:
Surround him with a blue and humid forest
Of damp attention. Not to disappoint
The father with images that are unwholesome, thoughtless,
Painter, help him who's everywhere with you,
Reasoning; feeling; always, always building.
Nor I nor anyone else, but all mankind, that's who—
Homer-Mankind will raise his praise's ceiling.
Painter, guard and preserve the warrior with your paint;
The woods of humanity sing after him, growing thicker—
The very future itself, the army of the sage—
They listen to him ever closer, ever quicker.

He leans over from the stage, as from a mount on high,
Into the mounds of heads. The debtor far surpasses
The suit against him: strictly kind the mighty eyes;
The thick eyebrow at someone nearby flashing;
And I would draw an arrow to point out
The firmness of the mouth—father of stubborn speeches;
The plastic, detailed eyelid, and about
Its outline, framing it, a million ridges;
He is all frankness, recognition, copper, and
A piercing earshot, which won't tolerate a whisper;
At everyone prepared to live and die like men
Come running playful somber little wrinkles.

Squeezing the charcoal in which all has converged,
And with a greedy hand seeking only a resemblance—
Trying to find only the resemblance's hinge—
I'll crumble up the coal, pursuing his appearance.
I learn from him, not learning for myself.
I learn from him to show myself no mercy.
And if unhappiness conceals the plan's great wealth,
I will discover it amid chaos and cursing.
Let me remain as yet unworthy to have friends,
Let me remain unfilled with tears and with resentment;
I still keep seeing him in a greatcoat, as he stands
In an enchanted square, with eyes full of contentment.

With Stalin's eyes a mountain is pushed apart.
The squinting plain looks far into the distance:
Like a sea without seams, the future from the past—
From a giant plow to where the sun's furrow glistens.
He smiles a reaper's smile, the smiling friend,
Reaper of handshakes in a conversation
Which has begun and which will never end
Smack in the middle of all of Creation.
And every single haystack, every barn
Is strong and clean and smart—a living chattel,
A mankind miracle! May life be large.
Listen to happiness's axis roll and rattle.

And six times over in my consciousness I keep,
Slow witness to the labor, struggle, and harvest,
His whole enormous path — across the steppe,
Across Lenin's October — to its kept promise.
Into the distance stretch the mounds of people's heads:
I become small up there, where no one will espy me;
But in kindhearted books and children's games, instead,
I'll rise again to say the sun is shining.
The warrior's frankness: there exists no truer truth.
For air and steel, for love and honor,
One glorious name takes shape on reader's tongue and tooth,
And we have caught it and have heard its thunder.

January — February 1937

◈ ◈ ◈

Like Rembrandt, martyr of light and shadow,
I have gone deep into the muteness of time
And the starkness of my burning rib
Is guarded neither by those warders
Nor by this warrior, who slumber in the storm.

Will you forgive me, splendid fellow,
Master and father of the black-green murk—
But the eye of the falcon feather
And the jewel box smoldering in midnight's harem
Trouble for no one's good—trouble and can but harm—
A tribe whose flame is billowed by twilight's bellows.

4 February 1937

◈ ◈ ◈

The curves of open coves, the pebbles, and the blue,
And the languid sail that continues in a cloud—
I am cut off from you, having hardly known your worth—
Longer than organ fugues, how bitter is sea grass,
That lies like hair and smells of lingering lies,
While iron languor makes the head mellow
And rust gnaws gently at the shallow shore…
So why have other sands been laid beneath my head?
You, guttural Urals, you, broad-shouldered Volga,
Or these here level lands — these are my only rights —
And with my whole chest I must still inhale them.

4 February 1937

I sing when my throat is wet, my soul is dry,
My vision damp enough, my mind not too too clever.
Is the wine wholesome? Are the wineskins sound?
Does my blood quicken with Caucasian fervor?
And my chest tightens — untongued — quieted:
Not I sing now — it is my breath that is singing —
My hearing stowed away, my head gone deaf…

A song not sung for gain is a tribute to itself —
Gall to an enemy, and a delight to friends.

A one-eyed song that grows out of the moss —
A monody, the gift of a life of hunting —
Sung in the saddle and in high places
With the breath held free and open
And with but one duty: to deliver
The young free of sin to their wedding.

8 February 1937

◊ ◊ ◊

Armed with the vision of the subtle wasps
That suck on the earth's axis, the earth's axis,
I access everything that I have seen
And I rehearse it to no purpose.

And I do not draw, nor do I sing,
Nor do I drag the dark-voiced bow.
I only drink life in and take delight
In envying the mighty, cunning wasps.

Oh, would that I might also be compelled
By and by—sleep and death bypassing—
Pricked by the air and by midsummer warmth,
To hear the earth's axis, the earth's axis...

8 February 1937

◈ ◈ ◈

Into a lions' den and bondage I am cast
And I sink lower, lower, lower,
Under the leaven torrent of these sounds,
Stronger than lions, more potent than the Torah.

Your call—how near, how near it comes
To the nativity of the commandments—
The linking up of Oceanic pearls
And the chaste baskets of Tahitian women...

A continent, a landmass of a voice,
That overawes with what lies below singing!
No wealthy daughter's sweetly savage face,
O foremother, is worth your little finger.

My time is still unlimited: I, too,
Have accompanied the universe's rapture
Even as an organ in an undervoice
Accompanies a woman singing.

12 February 1937

VERSES ON THE UNKNOWN SOLDIER

1

Let this air be the one to witness it
With its heartbeats carrying far—
Even in dugouts, environing, virulent—
An outletless ocean, a gas.

How these stars are denunciatory!
They just have to keep staring—what for?
For passing judgment on the judge and the witness—
At this outletless ocean, this gas.

And the rain—that unfriendly sower,
That manna without a name—
Still remembers the crosses that dotted
This V-shaped battle line.

And the people, cold and feeble,
Will kill and starve and freeze,
While inside his renowned monument
The unknown soldier lies.

Teach me, you feeble swallow
Who have forgotten how to fly,
How without wings or a rudder
To abide this grave in the sky.

And for one Mikhail Lermontov
I will answer on all counts—
How a hole in the air gapes for man
And a grave fixes his slouch.

2

Like grapes in wriggling formations,
These worlds threaten our world.
They hover, like stolen cities,
Like golden slips of the tongue, accusations,
Like berries of a poisonous cold—
Expanding in tent-constellations,
A dripping fat of gold…

3

Through the ether, a decimalized
Light, whose rush is crushed in a ray,
Begins a numeric transparency
With rows of zeroes and pain.

And the field of fields brings a new field
In a crane's triangular flight—
The news comes in a light-dust update
Bringing yesterday's battle's light.

The news comes in a light-dust update:
"I'm not Leipzig, I'm not Waterloo,
Not the Battle of the Nations, I'm something new
And will light up the light of the world."

4

The mash and the hash of Arabia—
Light, whose rush is crushed in a ray—
And slanting its soles on my retina,
The ray stands up on my eye.

Millions killed inexpensively
Have made a path in the void.
Good night! And farewell to them
From the fortresses of the earth!

Incorruptible sky of the trenches,
Sky of large-scale, wholesale death,
After you, away from you, all-embracing one,
My lips rush in the dark —

Past the shell-holes, the ditches and barricades,
Above which he gloamed and loomed:
The sullen, pockmarked, and humiliated
Genius of upturned tombs.

5

The infantry is good at dying
And the chorus sings well in the night
Above Schweik's crushed smile
And the lance of Don Quixote
And the bird track of the knight.

And man is friends with the cripple—
There'll be work for the one and the other—
And a family of wooden crutches
Knocks about on the century's outskirts—
Hey, fraternity, planet earth!

6

Does the skull have to develop—
From temple to temple, forehead-wide—
So that through its dear eye sockets
Troops might be poured inside?

The skull develops from living—
From temple to temple, forehead-wide—
With the purity of its seams it teases itself,
Comes to light as a dome of consciousness,
Foams with thought, dreams about itself,
The cup of cups and the fatherland's fatherland,
With a starry stitch held together,
The cap of happiness—Shakespeare's father…

7

Clarity, perspicacity,
Rushes back home shaded red,
As if nightmares overloaded
Both skies with their pallid flames.

Only what is in surplus avails us.
A reckoning awaits—not a wreck.
And fighting for air to subsist on
Is no glory for others to seek.

And as I overload my consciousness
With a nightmarish being alive—
Aren't I drinking this brew by choice
And eating my head under fire?

Is this why they prepared a receptacle
For such charm in empty space—
So that stars, reversing their whiteness,
Could rush back home shaded red?
Do you hear, stepmother of the galaxy,
Night, what is going to take place?

8

Blood fills the aortas
And a whisper runs through the ranks:
"I was born in ninety-four,
I was born in ninety-two."
And as I squeeze in my fist
The outworn year of my birth
My bloodless mouth whispers:
I was born on the night from the second
To the third of January in one
Unreliable year and the centuries
Surround me with flames.

1–15 March 1937

◇ ◇ ◇

Maybe this is a point of mindlessness,
Maybe this is your conscience—this,
The knot of life, wherein we are recognized
And untied into that which is.

Thus life-surpassing crystals, cathedrals,
Are stretched onto ribs by light,
That painstaking spider, who gathers them
Once more in a single beam.

Beams of pure lines, grateful ones,
Steered by a quiet ray
Will join, will unite someday,
Like guests with their heads unbared —

Only not in the sky, but on earth,
Forming a house filled with song—
How not to harm, not to frighten them—
If only we live so long…

Forgive me for speaking out loud…
Read it quietly to me now…

15 March 1937

◇ ◇ ◇

I am lost in the sky — what to do?
He to whom it is near, reply!
Ringing out was easier for you,
You discuses, Dante's nine.

Nothing can take me from life. Its
Dream is: kill — then caress,
So that ears, eyes, and their orbits
Overflow with Florentine grief.

And those laurels with stinging caresses —
Lay them not on my brow.
But my heart — tear it up into ringing,
Into ringing pieces of blue…

And when I sleep — after serving —
In life to the living a friend,
It will echo deeper and higher —
The reply of the sky in my breast.

9–19 March 1937

◈ ◈ ◈

I am lost in the sky—what to do?
He to whom it is near, reply!
Ringing out was easier for you—
You discuses, Dante's nine—
Out of breath, out of black, out of blue.

If I am not ancient, not useless—
You, who stand over me,
If you are a cupbearer and tapster—
Give me force without idle foam
To drink to the rotating tower
Of reckless, wrestling blue.

Places blue, places black, starling places,
Declaring the deepest blue—
Vernal ice, ice of spring, ice supernal—
Clouds, the brawlers of charm—
Hush—a rain cloud!—being led by the reins.

9–19 March 1937

◇ ◇ ◇

So that sandstone—no stranger to raindrops
And wind—might preserve them within,
Many egrets and bottles in bottles
Were scratched into sandstone by kings.

Exemplary dog-heads embellished
In Egypt the government's shame,
Dead men were stuffed with rubbish,
And bric-a-brac pyramids remain.

How far from all that is my brother—
My singer not without sin—
Who sued for peace for his ashes—
I still hear your gnashing of teeth…

His weak-willed estate—he unwound it,
Two testaments' worth of yarn,
And he left, in parting, in chirping,
A world as deep as a skull.

The mischievous neighbored the Gothic
And he spat on spiderweb law:
Cocky schoolboy and thieving angel,
The incomparable Villon, François.

He's an outlaw in the choirs of heaven—
No dishonor to sit next to him—
And even when the world is ending—
Even then, skylarks will ring.

18 March 1937

◈ ◈ ◈

Blue island made great by potters,
Green Crete! Their gift has been baked
Into resonant earth: like dolphins,
Can you hear their fins underground?

This sea is remembered and present
In clay that was blessed with firing
And the vessel's authority
Has cracked into sea and eye.

Give me back what is mine, blue island,
Flying Crete, give me back my labor
And succor the fired vessel
From the breasts of the flowing goddess.

This took place and was sung in the blue,
Before Odysseus, long ago,
Long before food and wine
Were ever called "yours" and "mine."

So convalesce in radiance,
You star of the ox-eyed skies,
When chance itself is a flying fish—
And talking water says: "yes."

21 March 1937

◇ ◇ ◇

The Greek flute's theta and iota—
Unsated by word of mouth—
Beholden to no one, unmolded,
Ripened, repined, crossed rifts.

And it cannot be abandoned
Or quenched by clenching the teeth
Or nudged with the tongue into language
Or subdued by using the lips.

And the flutist will never rest easy:
He imagines that he is alone,
That he sculpted his native ocean
Out of purple clays long ago…

With whispers bright and aspiring,
As memory spurs his lips,
He is at pains to be sparing
And he parcels out sounds with thrift.

In his wake we shall not repeat him
By marring clay in our hands,
And when I was filled with the ocean
My own measure became mortal to me…

And my own lips are unlovely—
For murder grows from that root—
And I dwindle, unwillingly dwindle
The indifferent force of the flute.

7 April 1937

◇ ◇ ◇

The pear tree and the bird cherry have taken aim at me—
Their scattershot force strikes at me unfailingly.

Flower clusters of stars, stars of flower clusters—
What is this twin authority? Which inflorescence is trustworthy?

Could it be their thrashing, could it be their blossoming
That strikes the air so weightlessly, flails it with their unity?

And the double fragrance's sweetness has no permanence:
Straining and dragging—it is mixed and fragmentary.

4 May 1937

[POEMS TO NATALYA SHTEMPEL]

1

Slightly unlevel upon hollow ground
With loveliness in her uneven steps
She walks, springing a little bit ahead
Of her quick girlfriend and young man companion.
She is drawn forward by a constrained freedom
Born of a vivifying imperfection
And it may well be that a lucid guess
Would linger for a while in her steps—
About the fact that this springtime weather
For us is the foremother of the tomb,
And that it will begin this way forever.

2

There are women who belong to the raw earth,
Whose every footfall is resounding sobbing.
To escort the resurrected and to be the first
To greet the dead is their calling.
To demand tenderness from them is a crime
And to part with them is beyond our powers.
Today, an angel; tomorrow, a worm of the grave;
And the day after—nothing but a likeness…
Footsteps that passed by once, will pass away…
Flowers are immortal, the sky is all-embracing,
And all that is to be—only a promise.

4 May 1937

My thanks to Lena Nekludova for many excellent conversations about these translations, which made them grow better

I. B.

A NOTE ON MANDELSTAM'S POEMS

IN 1930, MANDELSTAM WROTE: "I have no manuscripts, no notebooks, archives. I have no handwriting, because I never write. I alone in Russia work from the voice." Mandelstam's manuscripts and notebooks have survived, but his statement about working from the voice is corroborated by witnesses. Here is how Viktor Shklovsky, Mandelstam's neighbor for a time in 1920, described him: "With his head thrown back, Osip Mandelstam walks around the house. He recites line after line for days on end. The poems are born heavy. Each line separately." And here is how Sergey Rudakov, a young critic who visited Mandelstam in exile in Voronezh, described him in 1935: "Mandelstam has a wild way of working... I am standing in front of a working mechanism (or maybe organism, also) of poetry... The man no longer exists; what exists is — Michelangelo. He sees and understands nothing. He walks around mumbling: 'Like a black fern on a green night.' For four lines, four hundred are uttered, literally... He does not remember his own poems. He repeats himself and, separating out the repetitions, writes what is new."

I wonder if this way of writing, which may well have been Mandelstam's practice from the beginning, might account for that rare acoustic quality which all his poems share, regardless of when they were written. From first to last, they are poems that contain no noise: their only accompaniment is silence. Composed of lines that were arrived at only after a hundred alternatives had been spoken out loud and pushed aside, they indeed feel "born heavy"— if this is understood to mean born pregnant, born already heavy with something yet unborn, an unborn meaning or another unborn poem. An echo of expectancy is audible even in Mandelstam's earliest poems. It unfolds around them in silence line after line, urging those who hear them — even if they hear them only in their minds while reading them in silence — to listen more closely.

It remains just as audible in his last poems. I think it was the most indelible quality of his poetic voice, which stayed with him from beginning to end, even as his voice learned to become open to stronger and longer-lasting inspirations.

Speaking of his own growth as a poet, Mandelstam always named Nikolai Gumilev as his mentor. Gumilev, an adventurer-poet, five years older than Mandelstam and a world traveler — and eventually a decorated hero of the First World War — was the originator of the Acmeist movement to which Mandelstam adhered in his youth. In a review of Mandelstam's first book (1914), Gumilev pointed approvingly to a change that occurs partway through the collection, when Mandelstam "opens the doors of his poetry to all the phenomena of life that live in time, and not only in eternity or in the instant." I think it likely that these words stayed with Mandelstam and that he himself understood his poetic development — and Gumilev's role in his life — in these terms, as an opening of the doors to what is more alive.

This collection of translations opens with a poem that Mandelstam wrote after learning that Gumilev had been shot. In August 1921, Gumilev was arrested for participating in a conspiracy to overthrow the government — the charge most likely fabricated, the conspiracy most likely nonexistent — and summarily executed, along with dozens of others. Mandelstam was in Tiflis, Georgia, at the time, staying in a house without running water, as Nadezhda Mandestam described it in her memoirs, but with a barrel in the yard that was regularly filled with water from a spring. "The coarse homespun towel that we brought from the Ukraine also found its way into the poem." The poet's death, the death of a friend and mentor, inspired a stark vision of the earth as a stage for a sacrifice.

Mandelstam returned to Gumilev in a poem written ten years later, "To the German Language," also included in this collection. Several years after Gumilev's death, Mandelstam stopped writing poems. During the second half of the 1920s, he wrote only prose. What "reawakened him" to poetry again in 1930, as his wife writes, "was a meeting with a young biologist, Boris Kuzin," with whom he formed a close friendship. Mandelstam himself wrote in a letter about Kuzin: "His personality permeates... the whole recent period of my work. To him and only to him I owe... the period of the so-called 'mature Mandelstam.'"

While "To the German Language" is dedicated to Kuzin, the figure whose image flits across its stanzas is Ewald Christian von Kleist, a minor German poet and cavalry officer of the eighteenth century, whose verses appear in the poem's epigraph. Yet behind both of these figures rises the enduring outline of a third, who was both an army officer-poet and the first friend to have awakened Mandelstam when he "slept without form or feature" two decades earlier—Gumilev. Commemorating Mandelstam's "second awakening," which marked not only his return to poetry in 1930 but also a far more fateful opening of the doors in his poetry "to all the phenomena of life that live in time," the poem looks back to the first.

While Gumilev was Mandelstam's mentor as a poet in human or spiritual terms, influencing his understanding of the relation between poetry and life, the poet who had the greatest influence on Mandelstam's understanding of the relation between poetry and language, in my view, was Velimir Khlebnikov. Writing about Mandelstam's and Khlebnikov's early days during poetry readings at the Stray Dog Cabaret before the First World World, a contemporary recalls Mandelstam, "as usual, talking,

talking, and... suddenly stopping. 'I can't go on,' he said, 'because in the next room Khlebnikov is being silent.'"

For some time in 1922, a few months before his death, Khlebnikov came for dinner every day to the Mandelstams', who shared their food rations with him. As Nadezhda Mandelstam recounts: "such attentive care as Mandelstam showed for Khlebnikov, he never showed for anyone." One more anecdotal detail will illustrate the connection between the two poets. In March 1938, leaving for the sanatorium that would soon become the scene of his final arrest, Mandelstam took with him a volume of Dante, a volume of Pushkin, and the collected works of Khlebnikov (as well as the poems of Shevchenko, given to him as a present at the last minute).

What did Mandelstam learn from Khlebnikov? He answers this question himself very straightforwardly in his "Remarks on Poetry," written in 1923. "Poetic artillery batteries talk to one another with volleys of fire," Mandelstam writes, punning on the most canonic name in Russian poetry, which derives from the Russian word for cannon, *pushka*, "completely unfazed by the indifference of the time that separates them. In poetry, it is always war... Commanders of roots, like commanders of troops, take up arms against one another. The roots of words wage war in darkness, depriving each other of nutriment and earthly juices."

How are we to understand "commanders of roots"? Khlebnikov envisioned poetry as being endowed with a power to affirm semantic resemblances between words that resemble each other phonetically. To dramatize this vision, he eventually imagined a whole mythology for language, in which primordial roots with primordial meanings—which were not etymological roots, but sounds that recurred as kernels in actual words—branched out over time into words whose meanings had no apparent connection, but whose family resemblances could nonetheless be brought out in poetry.

But one need hardly follow him into this story of linguistic origins to appreciate the fact that readers who have lived their whole lives with the words "canon" and "cannon"—and who, every time they see or hear one of these words, inevitably see or hear in it a phantom of the other—might come to associate them not just phonetically, but semantically also; so that the kernel of sounds which these words share becomes loaded in their minds with an indefinable meaning that is common to both. But though indefinable, this meaning is not inaccessible: one might expect it to be taken as more than just a pun, for instance, if one were to describe the great books of a country as the cannon of its language firing through history...

Or one can make the same point, but in a way that puts more emphasis on the poet's own ability to create new meanings: even where no overlap in meaning between phonetically overlapping words yet exists in anyone's mind except the poet's before the poem is written—since the phonetic similarities uncovered by Khlebnikov were indeed often far less familiar than the one I have just mentioned—the poet, by affirming such an overlap, can bring its intelligible meaning into being.

"At the risk of sounding too elementary," Mandelstam continues in the essay quoted above, "simplifying my subject as much as possible, I would describe the negative and positive poles in the state of poetic language as prolific morphological blossoming and the hardening of morphological lava beneath a semantic crust. Poetic speech is vitalized by the roaming, polysemic root." What Mandelstam learned from Khlebnikov was to pay attention to roaming, polysemic roots, those clusters of sounds in a language that are "proto-semantic"—not just pure sounds, yet not yet hardened into any particular meaning—clusters of sounds that remain open to many meanings and fluctuate easily among them.

In Khlebnikov, attention to what is proto-semantic in language was all-absorbing from the beginning. Of course, in itself sensitivity to potential semantic affinities between similar-sounding words was hardly anything new in poetry. One finds it in every line of Shakespeare or Pushkin. But Khlebnikov elevated it into the central trope of his work, singlemindedly prioritizing it over every other aspect of rhetoric.

The starting point of such a trope is the same as the starting point of a pun: but whereas a pun contents itself with a laugh, turning its back on any further significance that a coincidence of sounds might be imagined to have, Khlebnikov's approach was precisely to amplify this significance into material for poetry, a material with a unique semantic potency, drawing on a realm of meanings that everyone lives with, but that are impossible to talk about.

As Mandelstam wrote about Khlebnikov in the same essay: "He has marked out pathways for the language's development, transitional, intermediary ones, and this historically nonexistent trajectory in the destiny of Russian speech, realized only in Khlebnikov, has become preserved in his *zaum* [the "transensical" language of Khlebnikov's proto-semantic coinages], which is nothing other than transitional forms that have not yet had time to become covered over with the semantic crust of a rightly and righteously developing language."

This vision of language, and of poetry's relation to language, which Mandelstam was only able to describe discursively in this essay from 1923, finally found its way into a magnificent poem written by him over a dozen years later, "Not mine, not yours, but theirs..." The poem not only formulates the vision, but also incarnates it, inwardly alive with morphological blossoming.

While Khlebnikov's insights influenced Mandelstam early on by informing his thinking about poetry, it was not until his exile in Voronezh (1935–1937) that Mandelstam came to assimilate them as skills, to incorporate them fully into his own voice. As he wrote in a letter about another poem composed shortly after "Not mine, not yours, but theirs…": "In this piece, employing very modest means, I have used the letter 'shch' and something else to make a (material) lump of gold. The Russian language is capable of miracles if only the poem obeys it, learns from it, and boldly wrestles with it. How every language honors a poet's wrestling with it, and with what coldness it repays indifference and feeble subordination!"

I have not attempted to translate the alchemy referred to here—the gold that Mandelstam made out of the sound "shch," though real, is not fungible, not least because this sound does not even exist in English. But the approach has become indistinguishable from Khlebnikov's, though the voice remains purely Mandelstam's, with all the acoustic qualities I described at the beginning of this note.

This is true of all the poetry Mandelstam wrote in Voronezh. In the poems written during these years, particularly during his last half-year there, one still recognizes Mandelstam's aspiration to compose poems that feel born heavy with unborn meanings. But now this aspiration has become combined with such caring attention to the "polysemic root" as Mandelstam had never shown before. The outcome is like nothing else in Russian poetry. From this last half-year come half the poems in this collection.

Mandelstam confronted Khlebnikov's ideas not only in prose during the 1920s, but also in poetry, as can be seen from two poems from 1922: "I know not when / This little song began" and "Up a little ladder I climbed." Both of them branch off from a short poem by Khlebnikov, which begins: "A little song [*pesenka*] is a little ladder [*lesenka*] into another heart" (1921). In these poems, Mandelstam contemplates a poet's role with respect to meanings already contained in language independently of the poet—whose only task might be to stir up language so that its inherent meanings, however incoherent, begin to resonate—and draws two opposite conclusions, one in favor of and one against such an approach to poetry. The subject of both poems is that *lesenka* which is also a *pesenka*, that ladder which is also a little song: a musical scale.

Mandelstam filled his poems with deliberate ciphers during these years. The mosquito-prince in the first poem is immediately recognizable to Russian ears as Prince Gvidon from Pushkin's "The Tale of Tsar Saltan," who becomes transformed into a mosquito in the tale. Grigory Amelin and Valentina Morderer, who wrote what in my opinion is the best and most imaginative book ever written about Mandelstam's poetry, *The Worlds and Collisions of Osip Mandelstam* (2001), have marvelously solved the riddle of Prince Gvidon: the tinkling mosquito-prince is Guido of Arezzo, the inventor of modern musical notation, who named the notes of the musical scale...

The ambivalence toward Khlebnikov's approach to poetry expressed by the coupling of these two poems would resurface in some of the poems Mandelstam wrote during his last half-year in Voronezh—more about them below—although by then this particular ambivalence would feed into a broader ruefulness about poetry, which Mandelstam referred to in one poem as "the cause of all my troubles." But by the end of his Voronezh period, Khlebnikov had become a palpable presence in all of Mandelstam's work. In fact, I believe he can be identified directly as the hero of Mandelstam's poem about Prometheus, "Where are the bound and fastened moans?"

Greek tragedy is gone and cannot be brought back, Mandelstam writes in this poem, but in Khlebnikov language itself becomes an amphitheater whose raked strata are its "growing ages"—rising to their feet as a body of spectators who are themselves the performance. After years of living with Mandelstam's marvelous and mysterious epithets for the Greek tragedians—Aeschylus the freight mover (*gruzchik*) and Sophocles the woodcutter (*lesorub*)—I cannot help reading them as purely Khlebnikovian anagrams of the place names associated with Prometheus's punishment: Georgia (in Russian, Gruziya) and Mount Elbrus (which is named explicitly in a poem written during the same days as this one, "Today I'm in a spiderweb of light"). The "he" described as "an echo and a hello" in the last stanza is also called a "milestone," *vekha*, a word which is in fact a homonym of Khlebnikov's initials—V. Kh.—or *Ve Kha*, as these letters would be pronounced in Russian (this pun on his name occurs in Khlebnikov's own work).

But plays on words in Mandelstam's late poems, as in Khlebnikov's, do not sew themselves up into language games. Instead, they open out endlessly into more meaning. The way in which this happens can be seen in Mandelstam's great poem "Armed with the vision of the subtle wasps." This poem is based on an assonance between the Russian words for "wasp" and "axis"—*osa* and *os'*—which share as polysemic a root as anyone could ask for, since it also appears in the poet's own name, and in the name of his persecutor.

By boldly wrestling with this assonance, Mandelstam has opened it out into a generalization of his idea from "Not mine, not yours, but theirs…"—now taken beyond language, beyond the power that originates at its unarticulated core, to a vision of the core of reality itself. The "axis of the earth" that Mandelstam has in mind is temporal rather than spatial in nature. It is imagined as a core of reality with which the poet has no direct contact—being in direct contact with his own life only—and which he is able to access only indirectly—through the vision of whatever might be such mysterious entities as *are* in direct contact with it.

The verb in the phrase in this poem's second stanza which I have translated as "I drink life in" is *vpivayus'*. In connection with stinging insects, it means: "I pierce, I stick a stinger into." But read more literally, the verb and the phrase mean: "I drink myself into life." As there is just one vowel of difference in Russian between the verb "to drink," *pit'*, and the verb "to sing," *pet'*—and the link between these verbs is further prepared by the use of the latter two lines earlier—with a very slight sound change the phrase could also be read to mean: "I sing myself into life." "I only sing myself into life and take delight / In envying the mighty, cunning wasps." Compared to the axis of the earth, life is ephemeral stuff. Yet into this stuff the poet sings himself, which gives him the right to say, in a poem written a month later: "Nothing can take me from life" ("I am lost in the sky—what to do?" (1)).

This poem from a month later is one of two that begin with the same four lines and proceed from them upward, blueward, along two different paths. Both are among the most exalted poems that Mandelstam ever wrote and need no commentary from me. By the end of the second of them, however, the poet's exaltation becomes uncontainable and comes apart in Khlebnikovian "transense."

In its last stanza, the poet's gaze becomes filled with the sky, with notes of the deepest blue, and with clouds, which are unexpectedly called the "wrestlers of charm." *Obayanie* means "charisma, charm," but Mandelstam appears to derive this word—both here and in the "Verses on the Unknown Soldier"—from the word *oba*, "both," so that in his poetic lexicon it means something like "bothness" or "possession by both," referring of course to the eyes. The Russian word for "clouds," *oblaka*, itself becomes a Khlebnikovian kenning for the eyes, here and elsewhere in Mandelstam's poetry, since it too contains the same phonetic kernel. Are we in the sky or in the poet's gazing eyes? Semantic logic begins to lose its grip as phonetic webs take over. But in the next line, as if suddenly frightened, the poet cuts himself off: "Hush! A storm cloud is being led by the bridle." My own imagination — though given Mandelstam's ways, it is not as far-fetched as it might seem — is that this last word appears in the poem because it is a Russian translation of the German *Zaum*.

"Zaum" is not the only threat that makes Mandelstam fall silent here, of course: the storm cloud in the poem has a darker ominousness to it than any that could be imputed to language. Indeed, an ominous undercurrent runs through virtually all of the poems Mandelstam wrote in Voronezh (one hears it in the last line of the Prometheus poem, for instance, nor are the "mighty, cunning wasps" envisioned by the poet as harmless beings). But this maneuver with the German word demonstrates a broader approach to lexical choices on Mandelstam's part: his punning, like Khlebnikov's, did not stop at linguistic borders. Again and again, instead of using a word, Mandestam will translate this word into a foreign language (most often German or French, but also others) and then use a Russian homonym of the foreign word; or he will find a foreign homonym for his word and then translate that homonym into Russian (as in the example above).

I mention this fact to indicate not only what the translator of Mandelstam is up against, but also what Russian readers of Mandelstam must make sense of. Occasionally, Mandelstam shows his hand. "My head is deaf" — *golova glukha* — he writes in the poem "I sing when my throat is wet, my soul is dry..." which alludes to the singing and languages of the Caucasus. Five years earlier, in his prose work "Journey to Armenia," he had recorded: "Head in Armenian is *glukh'*, with a slight aspiration after the *kh* and a soft *l*."

On the other hand, translating Mandelstam's poems from Russian to English, I have repeatedly come across lexical choices in them that make more obvious sense in translation than they do in Russian. A felicitous example of such a back-and-forth between languages, for example, comes up in the poem "Like Rembrandt, martyr of light and shadow…" Rembrandt is proverbially the *master* of chiaroscuro, of course, not its *martyr*—Mandelstam probably had the French words *martyre* and *maître* in mind when he made the swap, but it sounds just as natural in English. In Russian, however, the two words are nothing alike, and the link between them is revealed only through translation.

Indeed, the two poems about the little ladder which is also a little song, which I discussed above, are themselves premised on a pun in another language: the Italian word *scala*, which is both a ladder and a musical scale. But it is hardly by coincidence that still other scales find their way into the second of these poems, which contains the lines: "Not with our own skin's scales— / Against the hair of the world we sing." In Russian, the word for the scales of the skin has no phonetic connection to the subject of the poem. Translated into English, the motivation behind this lexical choice becomes apparent.

But let me go back to the ambivalence Mandelstam expressed toward relinquishing control over the reins of meaning to language in this way during his years in Voronezh, when his own control over these reins became responsive to the urgings of language as never before. The late poem "The Greek flute's theta and iota…" is precisely about the pull of what is proto-semantic in language. Its subject is the irresistible music of the mouth—irresistible for the poet—the sound of that which precedes sense, which carries him wherever it happens to go, indifferent to the semantic consequences of its ripening and repining. But for the poet those semantic consequences are quite real, for murder (*gubit'*) comes from the same root as his own moving lips (*guby*), and poetic speech all too easily turns prophetic. Thus the poem concludes by becoming its own palinode.

Mandelstam's Greek flute—the vocal reed which, with a will of its own, produces this polysemic music and beguiles the person who touches its ventages—is in fact the flute of Marsyas, which was used by its owner to challenge the supremacy of coherent speech as embodied by the music of the lyre.

Or so the myth was reimagined by Mandelstam's close friend Benedikt Livshits in his early poem "The Flute of Marsyas" (1911)—which was also the title of his first book. Livshits (1886–1938), an interesting poet in his own right, is particularly interesting in connection with Mandelstam because of the enduring thematic and stylistic affinities in their work. To my ears, if there is a contemporary of Mandelstam's the lexical texture or "mouth feel" of whose poems most resembles Mandelstam's, it is Livshits. Nadezhda Mandelstam, dismissive about Livshits, quoted Mandestam as saying, "I learn from everyone, even Livshits," clearly to imply the opposite—but though Mandelstam was unquestionably the greater poet, it is far from obvious in which direction the influence went. Livshits's knowledge of classical antiquity, for instance, was deeper than Mandestam's, and his interest in it older.

In the early 1910s Livshits was one of the Futurists and saw himself as an acolyte of Khlebnikov's. "The Flute of Marsyas" was written before his association with them. But for Mandelstam, picking up on the image again a quarter of a century later, it was natural to see the music of Marsyas in connection with

Khlebnikov's and the Futurists' attitudes toward language. Since Livshits is little known in English, I will include a translation of his poem here.

THE FLUTE OF MARSYAS

So may it be. In lands flooded with sunlight
You overcame the Phrygian, Citharede.
But the most vicious among all your triumphs
Is unreliable. Marsyas's wounds

Are not to be forgotten. His bloody track
Runs through the ages. In the mists his scions
Arise, arise. Hear you that Phrygian din,
That unrepressed delirium in their paeans?

The flying lamiae still keep their distance
And still the heights are yours. But the flame is dying,
And over all the earth shackled in ice

In the hour of your death, fulfilling someone's
Nocturnal law, the spurned flute of Marsyas
Will begin singing with ill-omened voice.

I hear something of Livshits, too, in another poem with ancient Greek elements written by Mandelstam around the same time as "The Greek flute's theta and iota...": "Blue island made great by potters..." The imagined island consolidated entirely out of the works of potters might be Crete, might be the floating island Delos—the birthplace of Marsyas's rival—might be the sinking island Atlantis. But the sea surrounding it, from which the clay out of which it was made was drawn, is the same body of water as that which the flutist in the other poem imagines himself to have sculpted and which fills Mandelstam and overwhelms him at the poem's end: the proto-semantic sea of language. Those who have worked with clay obtained from that sea—clay in which that sea remains ever present—have molded and fired it into enough terra cotta to form a whole terra firma of their resonant artifacts. Under the light of the sun, the morphological lava has hardened into a semantic crust. But the sea keeps importuning it—is audible even inside it—and the fate of the island is far from certain.

Whatever meaning one makes out in Mandelstam's juxtapositions of these concepts, the images he uses to talk about words and culture are very reminiscent of those used by Livshits in poems written in the 1920s. I will include a translation of one here, written in 1919, as another suggestive point of reference for Mandelstam's text.

> There is in waking an eternal grievance:
> It is an exile, not an exodus,
> From dreams in which, transcending time, Atlantis
> Out of the waters shows itself to us.
>
> The dwellers of a shore that is no longer,
> Uncaring for whatever shores still are,
> Why is it we must modify our heartbeat
> At the same time we step inside the ark?
>
> And sing! And sing! Or can it really be that
> This cry shall become singing flesh once more —
> And from the ocean of the word shall surface
> A terra firma—living metaphor?

Livshits's writings are also and much more directly connected to a poem that Mandelstam wrote in the early 1930s, "Canzone." This poem is so obscure even in Russian that one must wonder whether any of its meaning can survive a translation into English. Yet I find that its buoyant main theme still comes across clearly. In the early 1930s, Livshits wrote a book of reminiscences about the early years of the Futurist movement, *The One-and-a-Half-Eyed Archer*—a marvelous text, in part a memoir and a history, in part a work on poetics and itself a prose poem. Mandelstam knew it well, and his "Canzone" is built up in part as a collage of images borrowed from the book or suggested by it.

Thus, I read the word "tomorrow" in its first line not only as an adverb, but also as a noun, the object of Mandelstam's vision, suggested by the very name of the Futurist movement. "A literary loser," Livshits writes, "I don't know how fame gets born. By washing up gradually, like Anadyomene out of the sea foam? Or in a volcanic eruption, like Athena from the head of Zeus? God knows how it happens." Literary fame—or glory, as I have translated it, since the Russian word is the same—is in fact the theme of Mandelstam's own tomorrow, announced in the second line of the poem. To describe the growing notoriety of the poets of the left, Livshits refers to various "indicators of the high price of Futurist stocks," punning on the Russian word *aktsiya,* which means both "stock" and "action" (here in the sense of public performance). It is possible that this pun was the seed from which grew Mandelstam's images of bankers and stockholders. Such borrowings continue throughout the poem.

But one lucid theme—the theme of a superior vision—holds these motley elements together. The superior vision in question is one of which poetry is the visual organ. The "bankers of the alpine landscape" and "the holders of the gneiss's mighty assets" are kennings for the binoculars that appear two stanzas later, which give whoever looks through them visual possession of what is far away and far greater in size than what is close at hand. But what are these peculiar binoculars themselves, this precious present from the psalmist to the foreseer? What else but poems? And the distance they bridge is not spatial but—like the distance bridged by investments and stock shares—temporal: whoever looks through them can see the glorious tomorrow of what these poems themselves will become.

Behind the geological imagery in Mandelstam's "Canzone" I hear Livshits's vibrant description of his first encounter with Khlebnikov's work. I would like to quote this passage at length, since it will shed light not only on this poem, but also on others in this collection, as well as on Khlebnikov himself and on the response to him of his contemporaries:

> And now—Khlebnikov's manuscripts refuted all constructions. Presently I began to feel that I was becoming detached from my planet and already observing it from the side.
>
> What I experienced during the first minute did not in the least resemble the experience of a person going up in an airplane at the moment when it leaves the ground.
>
> There was no taking wing.
>
> No freedom.
>
> On the contrary, my whole being froze in apocalyptic horror.
>
> If the dolomites, porphyry, and schists of the Caucasian mountain range had suddenly come alive before my eyes and, baring their teeth at me with the flora and fauna of the Mesozoic era, had moved toward me from all sides, it would not have produced a greater impression.
>
> For I beheld with my own eyes the language come alive.

> The breath of the pre-temporal word blew in my face.
> And I understood that I had been mute since birth.
>
> All of Dahl [the great, many-volume dictionary of the Russian language] with his countless locutions surfaced as a tiny island amidst the raging elements.
>
> They lashed at it, overturning with the roots upward those frozen linguistic layers on which we have been accustomed to step as on solid ground.

Through poetry, the geology of language—each wrinkle in its gneiss, enduring over time scales at which the poet's immediate surroundings become indiscernible—is brought into immediate focus. Through poetry, the poet finds a means to step out of his immediate surroundings, a means to escape.

Apart from the theme of a superior vision, there is a prominent Jewish theme that runs through the poem—with its references to money-lending, King David, and the enigmatic "commander of the Jews"—precisely tracing the arc of the poet's escape. This last figure has been persuasively deciphered by Amelin and Morderer as none other than the eighteenth-century Russian poet Gavriil Derzhavin, whom Mandelstam had already challenged on poetic grounds in the poem "The Slate Ode," more about which below. A statesman as well as a poet in the court of Catherine the Great, Derzhavin was appointed by the empress to look into troubles arising in parts of Belorussia. Derzhavin wrote a report, blaming everything on the local Jewish population. A year later, he followed this report with a broad proposal for the resettlement of the Jews of Belorussia, to be carried out under the auspices of a protectorate, which was to be overseen by him personally.

"Raspberry caresses" are caresses that one would rather live without, and the ironic "selah" addressed by Mandelstam to his putative protector is meant in the same sense as the Psalmist's use of the word — as Amelin and Morderer read it — to indicate a break, a stop, to the accompanying musicians. Why the poet would wish to escape from all putative protectors and leave the land of the Hyperboreans in the early 1930s is not difficult to fathom.

Escape is a recurring theme in several poems that Mandelstam wrote in the early 1930s. In "Canzone," the escape takes place through visual projection into the temporal distance, by means of that remarkable organ of vision which the poet discovers in his own voice. In the lovely poem "Lamarck," it takes place along a biological route, as Mandelstam imagines himself descending the evolutionary stairs to join more and more primitive life forms, which are not subject to the historical reality under which he must live. But in the end, alas, nature has raised the drawbridge that separates us from them, and we must remain the vertebrates we are, even though the spinal column of the age we live in — as Mandelstam wrote in his poem "The Age" a decade earlier — has been broken.

Mandelstam owed his interest in Lamarck to Boris Kuzin, the biologist who sparked his "second awakening" in 1930. Kuzin was a Neo-Lamarckian, and Mandelstam found Kuzin's ideas about biological evolution consonant with his own ideas about the creative process. He devoted many passages to this subject in his prose work "Journey to Armenia" (1932), in which Neo-Lamarckian conceptions of evolution and embryological development are formulated in ways that evoke the writing of poetry and inspiration:

> A plant is a sound elicited by a theremin wand, a warbling within a sphere oversaturated with fluctuating waves. It is an envoy of the living storm that rages perpetually

throughout creation—as akin to a rock as to a lightning bolt! A plant [the Russian word for plant literally means "a growing"] in the world is an event, a happening, an arrow—not boring old development!

And conversely, Mandelstam's characterizations of the cognitive efforts involved in the writing of poetry call to mind the growth of a living organism:

All of us, without suspecting it, are carriers of enormous embryological experience: the whole process of recognition, crowned by the triumph of the effort of memory, is remarkably similar to the phenomenon of growth. In both cases, there is a seedling, a germ, and—a facial trait or half a character, half a sound, the ending of a name, something labial or palatal, a sweet pea on the tongue, develops not out of itself, but merely responds to an invitation, merely stretches itself out, justifying an expectation.

The concepts of individual creativity, growth, and biological evolution blend together and become indistinguishable. As Mandelstam goes on to write in a section of "Journey to Armenia" entitled "Around the Naturalists," which draws on his readings of Lamarck, Linnaeus, Darwin, and others:

No one, not even hardened mechanists, regards the growth of an organism as the result of changes in the environment. That would be just too great an insolence. The environment merely invites the organism to grow. Its functions are expressed in a certain favorability, which is gradually and ceaselessly extinguished by an austerity that confines the living body and rewards it with death.

> Thus, for the environment an organism is a probability, a desirability, and an expectancy. For the organism, the environment is an inviting force. Not so much an outer skin as a provocation.
>
> When the conductor draws out a theme from an orchestra with his baton, he is not the physical cause of the sound. The flow of sound is already given in the score of the symphony, in the spontaneous accord of the performers, in the crowdedness of the hall, and in the design of the instruments.

The conceptual world we find ourselves in when reading these passages is very similar to the one evoked by Mandelstam ten years earlier when he spoke of an underground agon among polysemic roots whose tensions can be brought out into the light of day and captured in concrete meanings by an inspired wave of the poet's wand. Mandelstam's rhetoric has taken on a new biological coloring, but it is not hard to see why the ideas he was exposed to by Kuzin penetrated so easily into his own thinking.

Over the next two years, this thinking crystallized into a number of poems known collectively as the "Octaves," which do not constitute a poetic sequence, according to Mandelstam's testimony, but are the interconnected fragments of a single poem that was never written. Their shared theme is the creative process, as Mandelstam envisioned it, as it plays out in different manifestations of life. The theme's breadth is announced in the first poem, whose first stanza sums up the poet's personal experience of inspiration and whose second stanza envisions space itself as a metaphysical entity undergoing the same process.

The next two poems in the "Octaves" return to the creative process in the strict sense of the term, as it unfolds in the writing of poetry. The poem about the butterfly that follows—which has been nicely read by Amelin and Morderer as being about an unread book whose pages still need to be cut open, an image not foreign to Mandelstam's interests, in whose light the poem "Idle inside a mountain an idol dwells..." from the Voronezh period might also be read—mingles the theme of literary creativity with the biological theme of a butterfly emerging from a chrysalis. In subsequent poems, different facets of the same theme unfold amalgamatedly in the lexicons of architecture, geology, art, mathematics, and so on, until we end up in the penultimate poem—"Out of bowls full of pins and pestilence..."—peering at a slide through a microscope and observing what is only an "illusory causality."

In the last of the "Octaves"—"The neglected garden of magnitudes..."—the poet once again considers space as a metaphysical entity. Employing a mathematical vocabulary, he now affirms our ordinary understanding of causality to be imaginary—the notion that causes are invariant being as spurious as the notion that a wave of the conductor's baton will invariably produce the same sound. He abandons the idea of any space subject to such a causality, and steps into the real world of the actual values and magnitudes by which space is occupied, which are infinitely in the process of becoming, growing, evolving. In this real world, this neglected garden, the supposed permanence and self-identity of causes appear as ephemeral as leaves on plants—the poet easily plucks them off, and declares his intention to consider only the roots that are left.

The meaning of this intention is very close to the message of the poem "Not mine, not yours, but theirs..." from a couple of years later. But its formulation here makes it sound more like a conceptual riddle than a mysterious vision. The same may be said of many of the "Octaves," all of which seem to point from different angles to the same central concept, which remains so multidimensional that it cannot be grasped by any one of them, but is only revealed piecemeal.

Conceptual density, in fact, is an abiding characteristic of Mandelstam's work. While I have talked about Gumilev's influence on Mandelstam's understanding of poetry's openness to life, and about Khlebnikov's influence on his understanding of poetry's openness to language, I have not said much about the nature of Mandelstam's actual inspiration. Whom was the poet praying to, if anyone? Nor do I intend to say much about this, leaving readers to draw their own conclusions, except to point out that a fundamental quality of his inspiration was its conceptual density. The "Octaves" invite readers to contemplate the concepts they depict, to weigh Mandelstam's choices of words and images from a philosophical perspective as much as from any purely poetic one. The same is true of the great majority of Mandelstam's poems. At times, the conceptual side of a poem overwhelms everything else in it — as it does, to my ears, in some of the "Octaves." At other times, the balance is just right, and the passage between turning poetry into thought and turning thought into poetry remains free and open. An outstanding characteristic of Mandelstam's Voronezh period is that such freedom and openness is sustained within all the poems he wrote during those years.

I will conclude these notes, in part to illustrate the kind of attention to their details that the conceptual density of Mandelstam's poems stimulates, with stanza-by-stanza readings of two poems written by him during his last months in Voronezh, two poems in which he returns to the great tradition inaugurated in European poetry by Dante in the *Paradiso* — the tradition of poetry about light. But before I do that, I would like briefly to touch on several other poems included in this collection, a few of Mandelstam's most important poems among them, to provide readers with some points of reference for my translations.

🙢

In no work of Mandelstam's is conceptual density more in evidence than in the long poem in which he opposed Derzhavin not by means of a sly historical allusion, as in "Canzone," but as one poet openly challenging another: "The Slate Ode." Written in 1923, "The Slate Ode" is Mandelstam's hermetic *ars poetica*, his extended response to eight lines which Derzhavin wrote down on a writing slate three days before his death, sometimes published under the title "On Corruptibility" (1816):

> The river of time in its rushing current
> Bears all the affairs of men away
> And drowns in the abyss of oblivion
> Nations, kingdoms, and kings.
> And if through sounding lyre and trumpet
> Something does happen to remain,
> Then by eternity's maw devoured
> It will not dodge the common fate.

In eight stanzas filled with clashing lexical textures and greatly compacted metaphors, Mandelstam presents a poetic argument intended to prove that, through poetry, running water from the river of time can be made to flow back into the enduring rock of the writing slate — its course along the bent U of the horseshoe closed into the O of the ring. Alert to both the fleeting days and the eternal night, the poet learns from both, and the sediments of light and darkness in his writings, under pressure from his attention and inspiration, become a single metamorphic essence — triumphantly held up by Mandelstam in the face of Derzhavin's pessimism.

Mandelstam's grand syllogism, if brought into focus, can be exciting to read in Russian, and I hope to have transmitted some of that excitement in English. To let just a little air into its forbidding density, I should mention that the Russian word for slate is a loan word from the German *Griffel*, which sounds very close to "griffon" and gives rise to a series of phonetically motivated bird images in the poem. Hence, the "shrieking of the slate stone" on a precipice above the rushing current.

I will say a word about two poems of Mandelstam's that were as much political acts as they were poems, one of which is included in this collection. Joseph Brodsky, with "The Slate Ode" in mind, astutely rechristened Mandelstam's notorious ode to Stalin — which begins: "If I were to take up charcoal for highest praise…" — as his "Charcoal Ode." A great deal has been written about this poem, which indeed bears some monstrous kinship to the laudatory odes written by Derzhavin to Catherine the Great, but to me the outstanding fact about it remains that it is the only serious poem written in praise of Stalin by any major Russian poet who lived under him. Many poems in praise of Stalin were written during this period, of course, including by major poets. But none of them have endured as poetry. This one has, and will.

Remarkably, the only serious poem written as an explicit attack on Stalin by any major Russian poet who lived under him, to the best of my knowledge, was also written by Mandelstam. That poem is his famous "Stalin epigram" (1933, not included in this collection), which begins: "We live unaware of the land underfoot…" and of which Boris Pasternak said that it was not a poem, but a suicide, when Mandelstam recited it to him.

One wonders if it was Mandelstam's desperate need to open the doors of his poetry to all the phenomena of life that live in time, and not only in eternity or in the instant, that impelled him to make both poems as powerful as they are. Although each of them had a pragmatic purpose behind it — in one case, a suicide attack, in the other, an attempt at redemption — each endures indepedently of its motivation, as a work of art.

The ode to Stalin was the first Mandelstam poem I translated, years before I attempted any of the others, and my translation was a prank: I wanted to try something I called "simultaneous translation of poetry," which involved translating a poem as quickly as possible and taking any liberties necessary, while sticking as closely as possible to the rhyme and meter scheme of the original. The translation of the Stalin ode in this collection is the result of that exercise. I have included it because it seems to work as a poem, if read briskly, and because it seems to me in retrospect that doing it as a prank was the proper way to translate a poem which in some strange way was itself a prank — or maybe an anti-prank, if one can imagine such a thing, a prank played on oneself…

In the same month when he started writing the Stalin ode, January 1937, Mandelstam composed a quatrain about "an outcast poem": "As a celestial stone awakens the earth somewhere…" I have never been able to determine which of the two poems these lines refer to: the Stalin epigram, for which Mandelstam himself was sent into exile, or the Stalin ode, a misbegotten outcast among Mandelstam's poems (so it was seen, for example, by Nadezhda Mandestam, who did not want it published with the rest of her husband's work, although she preserved it). I used to think it was the latter, but now I'm inclined to believe it was the former.

The swing from one extreme to another which is embodied in these two poems about Stalin exemplifies an irrepressible characteristic of Mandelstam's personality, his rashness. Mandelstam himself was not blind to this aspect of his temperament and, in one of his Voronezh poems, left a wonderful portrait of himself in a momentary fit of rage. Depicting himself as a goldfinch confined within a cage of calumny, Mandelstam puts me in mind of Lady Macduff's son, who, when asked by his mother, "How will you live?" explains to her, "As birds do, mother," right before both are killed.

The word "calumny," *kleveta*, has a fraught history in Russian poetry, beginning with its use by Pushkin in the title of the poem "To the Calumniators of Russia," addressed to French politicians and writers who remonstrated against the crushing of the Polish Uprising of 1831 by the Russian army. Mandelstam's goldfinch poem, in which the polysemic root of *kleveta* ramifies into *kletka,* "cage," and implicitly into *klyuv,* "beak," could likewise be given the title "To the Calumniators of Russia," but with the "of" now understood subjectively rather than objectively, as addressing not those who calumniate the country, but the innumerable calumniators who inhabit it. They are the ones who form the hundred spokes of the cage around Mandelstam, who form the very perch that his goldfinch must balance on, and the whole world outside the cage is populated by them also, so that contrary to the usual state of affairs there is no freedom anywhere in the world outside the cage, and the only place where freedom can be found is in the space of the goldfinch himself, on the inside — thus, "everything in the world is inside out." "Salamanca" sounds as alluring in Russian as it does in English, but that is indeed because it calls to mind the word *primanka*, "lure," as well as the word *silok*, "bird snare," and it becomes clear what "universities" for clever, disobedient birds in the forests of the Soviet Union are being referred to in the poem.

Mandelstam left many other self-portraits in his poems from Voronezh. He also wrote a number of poems in which he imagined himself dead. One of the earliest among these is "What street is this? / This is Mandelstam Street..."—a little poem which, with its catchy rhymes and rhythms, could have been written for children, were it not so grim.

Significantly, the line from which this entire poem derives was suppressed by Mandelstam in its written version, for obvious reasons. One of the streets on which the Mandelstams found themselves living in Voronezh was Lenin Street. "He lived on Lenin Street," according to Nadezhda Mandelstam, was originally the third line of the second stanza. Even as he imagined a pit for himself, Mandelstam asserted that his name would outlive that of the founder of the country.

The theme of his poetry's durability reappears in another poem in which Mandelstam imagines himself dead, which is his variation on the classic statement of this theme by Horace—or rather, on its reformulation by Pushkin. The poem "Yes, I lie in the earth, moving my lips..." belongs to a tradition in Russian poetry of translations and rewritings of Horace's *Exegi monumentum*, which had first been translated by Mikhail Lomonosov in 1747 and then rewritten by a whole succession of poets, whose versions referred to their predecessors' in Russian more than to the Latin original. The most famous of these rewritings, which indeed became a poem repeated by every schoolboy in Russia, is Pushkin's from 1836:

I have raised a monument to myself not made by hand.
The people's path to it shall not become overgrown.
It has uplifted its unruly head higher
Than Alexander's column.

No, all of me will not die — my soul in the sacred lyre
Will outlive my ashes and avoid decay
And glory shall be mine as long as in the sublunary world
At least one poet remains.

Bleakly reimagining Pushkin's monument in 1935, Mandelstam places himself underground, the earth bulging above him, the bulge stretching out over the earth.

Mandelstam would go on to envision himself as dead most memorably in "Verses on the Unknown Soldier." That orchestrally complex and discordant work, composed shortly after the ode to Stalin, was pronounced an oratorio by its maker — his *Apocalypsis cum Figuris*. It concludes with a roll call of the dead, among whom the poet numbers himself.

During the last year of Mandelstam's exile in Voronezh, he and his wife became friendly with a young woman named Natalya Shtempel, for whom Mandelstam wrote two poems that he described, after reciting them to her, as "the best thing I've written."

There are women who belong to the raw earth,
Whose every footfall is resounding sobbing.
To escort the resurrected and to be the first
To greet the dead is their calling.

Who is the resurrected? Who is the dead? Of course, it is Mandelstam himself — already dead during his life, and beckoning his listener to be the first person to greet him as such; already resurrected during his life, again in her company. But death and resurrection do not follow their usual order: we are shown the poet first as newly resurrected, by means of this poem, and only after this for the first time as dead, also by means of this poem. This is not the death of one who dies namelessly among the many; neither is it a death that leaves behind a monument or an impossible street name; rather, it is the death-in-life of a poet and its proper realm poetry itself.

Natalya Shtempel walked with a limp, hence the opening lines of the first of the two poems dedicated to her:

> Slightly unlevel upon hollow ground,
> With loveliness in her uneven steps,
> She walks, springing a little bit ahead
> Of her quick girlfriend and young man companion.

The young man and woman mentioned in the fourth line were simply friends of Shtempel's with whom she and Mandelstam had gone out walking on a May night shortly before Mandelstam wrote this poem, but I like to imagine that "her quick girlfriend" and "young man companion" referred also with a sweet-and-sad smile to Shtempel's other friends — Mandelstam and his wife themselves.

Coda: Two Poems about Light

Mandelstam was not the first person to compare the retina to a spiderweb — the Greek anatomist who first described this body part had given it the name *arachnoides* — but he was perhaps the first poet to envision himself in the midst of photoreceptive tissue, surrounded by luminous filaments and experiencing a clarity in which even the needs of the nation become viewable. In the poem "Today I'm in a spiderweb of light…" from 1937, he returns to the concept of poetry as a sensory organ allowing for a superior vision, first formulated in "Canzone" five years earlier. Poetic saying is what enables seeing, rather than the other way around, and the ideal poem must be the psalmist's gift to the visionary.

In his youth, Mandelstam compared the poetic word to a stone, and he revives this image in the poem's second stanza, only now he knows what kind of stone it must be: one that is endowed with the faculty of vision, one that is capable of tears… and such stones not even the expanse and geological variety of Soviet lands can boast of.

Finally, in the third stanza, Mandelstam lays old metaphors aside and says directly what this poem is about: it is a poem about a poem, one that could become an ever-open eye for the people, ensuring their wakefulness. Only the filaments out of which its retina would be spun would be made not of light, but of its own sound, which would wash those who see through it in the manner of lachrymation.

In a poem composed a couple of months later, "Maybe this is a point of mindlessness," Mandelstam's attention shifts from the spiderweb to the spider who spins it. The starting point is once again the eye, through which we are simultaneously grasped by others and unbound into waking life ourselves. The poem's second stanza repeats this figure, now not from our point of view, but from the point of view of light, imagined as a busy little spider. Spinning a retina out of rays that issue out of itself, it sends these filaments out into the world, to render objects visible, and collects them again in a bundle when they are reflected back into the eye. The eye, considered from this angle, is simply an intrusion by light into human anatomy, a convergence of its multiple rays in a single bundle or beam.

It is in the third stanza of this poem that Mandelstam embarks on a description of a mysterious process in which multiple such bundles, shown the way by a ray, themselves undergo a still further bundling, to form what he compares to "a music-filled house." What is he describing in this beautiful image of light guiding light? He is describing human eyes being led by the light of day toward a shared focusing. What will be the common object of their attention? What can it be but a poem: not one spoken out loud, but one that appears on a page, where readers' eyes gather across the ages in silence. This is why the ray that facilitates their concentration is given the epithet "quiet": because it plays a role in a context in which out-loudness might have been expected. But across the ages a poem survives only on the page, in the written word, voicelessly. Yet notice the contrast between the silence in which the steering, the gathering, and the reading take place, and the music that fills the house once the guests who form it arrive.

Finally, who is the addressee of the last two lines?

> Forgive me for speaking out loud...
> Read it quietly to me now...

The reappearance of the word "quietly" gives it away: I believe it is to the bundles of light in his own eyes that Mandelstam offers this apology for using his voice, lest it disturb the process envisioned in the preceding stanzas.

List of Titles and First Lines in Russian